CUTTING-EDGE TECHNOLOGY

DRONES

Louise and Richard Spilsbury

Gareth Stevens
PUBLISHING

Please visit our website, **www.garethstevens.com**.
For a free color catalog of all our high-quality books,
call toll free 1-800-542-2595 or fax 1-877-542-2596.

Cataloging-in-Publication Data

Names: Spilsbury, Louise.
Title: Drones / Louise and Richard Spilsbury.
Description: New York : Gareth Stevens Publishing, 2017. | Series: Cutting-edge technology | Includes index.
Identifiers: ISBN 9781482451627 (pbk.) | ISBN 9781482451566 (library bound) | ISBN 9781482451443 (6 pack)
Subjects: LCSH: Drone aircraft–Juvenile literature.
Classification: LCC UG1242.D7 S65 2017 | DDC 623.74'69–dc23

First Edition

Published in 2017 by
Gareth Stevens Publishing
111 East 14th Street, Suite 349
New York, NY 10003

© 2017 Gareth Stevens Publishing

Produced for Gareth Stevens by Calcium
Editors: Sarah Eason and Harriet McGregor
Designer: Simon Borrough
Picture researcher: Rachel Blount

Picture credits: Cover: Getty Images: PHILIPPE HUGUEN (photo), Shutterstock: Eky Studio (banner), Shutterstock:
R-studio (back cover bkgrd); Inside: AeroVironment, Inc.: 6, 19; senseFly Ltd: 41; Shutterstock: Avarand 39, Boscorelli
25, ChameleonsEye 36, Steve Collender 35, Maria Dryfhout 11, Igor.stevanovic 17, Istanbul_image_video 12,
Ivan_Sabo 33, Jbor 44, Alexander Kolomietz 5, Lucky Business 9, Marekuliasz 28, Slavoljub Pantelic 43; Wikimedia
Commons: Cargyrak (CC BY-SA 4.0) 1, Erik Hildebrandt 27, Jrfreeland 21, Jessica Lea/DFID (CC BY 2.0) 33, U.S. Air
Force Staff Sgt. Christopher Matthews 22, U.S. Air Force photo by Bobbi Zapka 15.

Printed in the United States of America
CPSIA compliance information: Batch #CS16GS: For further information contact Gareth Stevens, New York, New York at 1-800-542-2595.

CONTENTS

CHAPTER 1

DRONES

Have you ever looked up to watch birds, insects, helicopters, or airplanes moving through the air? Imagine if the skies of the future were filled with flying objects that were neither living nor had pilots inside. This idea is not far from reality. Aerial robots called drones exist, are used in many industries, and are here to stay!

UNMANNED VEHICLES

A drone is an unmanned aerial vehicle (UAV). It has its own power source and can either fly alone or can be operated by a pilot on the ground by remote control. A drone can carry objects ranging from cameras to weapons. So far a drone sounds a little like a radio-controlled airplane. But the big difference is that drones have computers on board that enable them to automatically adjust and correct how they fly. The ability to do things on their own requires computer **programming**. Drones are partly **autonomous** robots.

GLOBAL DRONES

There is a huge variety of different drones in use worldwide today. Some of us might think that drones are entirely used in the military for keeping watch on an enemy or for dropping bombs on them. However, drones are used for many other equally important tasks. They monitor populations of endangered animals or the health of crops. They spot forest fires or monitor crowds of protestors to keep them safe. Drones are used to search for survivors of accidents, to help make maps, and to shoot movies. They are also great toys!

Drones are flying robots that are operated from the ground by radio control, but also by inbuilt computers that help them control their own flight.

OTHER NAMES

"Drone" was first used to mean pilotless military airplanes that towed targets for soldiers to get some shooting practice. Now that there are other types of drone, some people want to use other names for them that are unconnected to the military. In addition to UAVs, they might use remote piloted aircraft (RPA) or unmanned aerial system (UAS).

DRONE HISTORY

In the early twentieth century, inventors dreamed of unmanned airplanes fighting battles. However, UAVs remained a dream until the late 1950s.

SAFER AERIAL MISSIONS

The U.S. Air Force began to develop UAVs in the Vietnam War to help reduce the loss of human lives during battles and to avoid pilots being caught by the enemy. These vehicles were based on the Firebee target drones that had been used since the early 1950s. These were small, unmanned airplanes with powerful engines. They often launched from under the wings of large airplanes. The newer Firefly UAVs had bigger wings and tails, and more powerful engines so they could fly faster and farther. They could get above enemy territory and take photographs of the opposition.

The small drones of the present developed partly from big military drones used in the Vietnam War.

DRONE IMPROVEMENT

The cameras on the Fireflies parachuted to Earth for soldiers to collect the photographs, but many cameras were lost. By the 1970s, the Israeli Air Force had developed drones with video cameras that could transmit images to troops on the ground. The drones could fly low, like airplanes, so enemy missiles targeted them rather than manned airplanes. In the 1990s, sophisticated U.S. UAVs such as the Predator drone entered combat in the Gulf War. These modern drones could navigate themselves and fire missiles of their own. Since then, UAVs have been used in conflicts worldwide. Advancements in drone technology made by the military have been used to create stable, unmanned flying machines used for a wide variety of nonmilitary applications.

COMBAT

In December 2002, for the first time in history, a drone took part in a dogfight, or aerial battle, against another airplane. An Iraqi MiG fighter-jet fired a missile at a U.S. Air Force Predator drone and the drone pilots on the ground made it fire a missile back. The Predator was destroyed and the MiG escaped. This event proved that drones controlled from the ground at that time could not fly as fast, maneuver (move) as well, or match the weaponry of modern airplanes.

Today's drones are a regular part of a lot of air forces and standard equipment for many industries. However, they are still relatively new to the skies and people are debating their pros and cons.

PROS

Cost: It is much less expensive to buy a drone to do a task, such as taking photographs of an area, than hiring a helicopter and crew to do it for you. A drone may cost $1,000 to buy and a little more to train its users, but the equivalent helicopter service might cost $1,000 per hour!

Safety: Flying a drone from the ground is much safer than piloting an airplane, especially for military use.

Speed and maneuverability: Many drones cannot fly as fast as airplanes but it is often much quicker to deploy them, or move them into position, ready for action, than it is to deploy an airplane. This is partly because they are generally smaller, easy to transport, and do not need to launch and land at designated airports. Drones can also fly closer to objects than helicopters and move around them more easily.

CONS

Safety: Even small drones can cause injury or even death if they malfunction and crash into people on the ground, manned aircraft, or infrastructure such as electrical wires.

Jobs: Using drones instead of people for anything from surveying to agriculture can mean that people lose their jobs.

Privacy: People have the right to remain private and this right is affected if there are a lot of drones taking photographs of them and their activities.

DRONE PILOTS

In 2011, the U.S. military trained more drone pilots than actual fighter pilots! Today, fewer U.S. military drone pilots are trained each year because they fly more hours than a regular pilot and are paid less. However, experts think that between 2016 and 2025, the drone industry may create 100,000 jobs. This includes people who make, maintain, and control drones.

Drones are very adaptable and user-friendly robots that can be operated by people with only basic piloting skills from a wide variety of locations.

CHAPTER 2

TYPES OF DRONES

Drones come in different shapes and sizes, and can look like helicopters or airplanes. Drones can only stay in the air and move through it by overcoming and balancing the **forces** that act on them.

FLIGHT FORCES

Gravity is a force that pulls anything down toward Earth. Lift is a force that pushes things upward. An airplane can only stay in the air if lift is greater than gravity. Drones create lift using wings or propellers that spin horizontally. They move forward or backward using the force of thrust. This is produced either by jet engines or propellers that spin vertically. A backward push called **drag** resists thrust. It is caused by the air through which a drone moves. A drone can only move if its thrust is greater than drag.

CONTROLLED FLIGHT

A drone's power source is often an onboard battery. The battery powers its motors, which spins the propellers. Larger drones can have engines that use fuel to provide thrust and lift. The power source is controlled partly by the operator on

CUTTING EDGE

Today's drones can hover in one spot and land in the same spot from which they took off using fixed **global positioning system (GPS)** coordinates. New drones can find safe places to land without GPS. They use a downward pointing camera and ultrasonic **sensors** to map the land below and identify safe, flat land sites!

lift

thrust

drag

gravity

A drone can only fly properly if its operator on the ground and flight controller instruct its motors to produce the right balance of forces.

the ground using instructions sent as radio waves. But drone flight is also controlled automatically by an inbuilt computer called a flight controller. The flight controller is programmed with information on how to fly, and it also reacts autonomously depending on **data** from onboard devices. **Gyroscopes** and **accelerometers** sense the drone's position and speed. An **altimeter** figures out the drone's height above the ground. Using the data, the controller can speed up or slow down the motor to vary lift and thrust, and adjust the drone's course.

Most toy and commercial drones have **rotors**, which are sets of propellers spaced around their centers. Rotors allow them to hover and move in different directions.

BLADES AND ROTORS

Helicopters usually have one horizontal rotor made up of several propeller blades, but drones are multicopters. They can be quadcopters with four rotors, hexacopters with six, or octacopters with eight. Each rotor usually has two blades. If one rotor motor fails, the others can easily keep the drone up and stable in the air. Each rotor can be small, which leaves more space in the center of the drone to carry its **payload**.

You can see how the pair of blades making up a drone rotor are angled differently to create maximum lift.

PROPELLERS AND FLIGHT

In a multicopter drone, rotors are arranged around the center on stalks. Each rotor spins in the opposite direction to those on its right and left, and in the same direction as the rotor diagonally opposite to it. Balancing the directions of spin gives the drone stable flight. The controller can adjust the direction and speed of the drone by altering the speeds of all the different rotors. For example:

- To move upward, the rotors must speed up and provide more lift.
- To move down, the rotors must slow down and provide less lift.
- To hover in one spot, all rotors must spin at the same speed.
- To move forward, the rotors at the back of the drone must slow down and those at the front speed up.

BIRDS

The wings of a soaring eagle have a curved shape with a thicker leading edge and a thinner, tapering back edge. This wing shape is called an aerofoil. When an aerofoil moves along, air travels above and below the wing. The air has to move farther and faster over the top to meet with air beneath. The faster air above has less pushing power than the slower air beneath, so it lifts the aerofoil. The rotors of a multicopter have propeller blades with an aerofoil shape to provide lift as they spin around.

DRONE PLANES

The appearance of some drones is similar to a regular airplane. Instead of rotors for lift, drone planes have a pair of long, aerofoil-shaped wings. While they move forward, the wings provide lift and keep them in the air.

STAYING UP

Drone planes have long, narrow wings. These give lift and are lightweight. The narrow shape also creates less drag. The source of thrust in drone planes can be a rotor powered by an engine or batteries, or it can be a jet engine. Jet engines burn fuel inside to make hot gases that push backward on the air and speed the drone forward. Plane drones change altitude, or height, using vents that change the direction of the gases that come out of the jet engine.

CHANGING DIRECTION

Some drone planes, such as the Global Hawk drone, have long flaps called ailerons on the trailing, or back, edges of its wings that can move up or down. When the aileron on one wing rises, it artificially makes the top of the aerofoil longer and creates more lift in that wing. Lowering an aileron on the other wing has the opposite effect. The different lifts on each wing make the drone angle to one side and turn in the air. On the Predator drone, the wings have no ailerons. Instead, it has a vertical **rudder** beneath that can angle left or right. Air flowing past the moving drone pushes on one side or another making it change direction. The v-shaped tail wings next to the rudder help keep the drone stable in the air. They also act as stands when the drone lands, keeping the propeller at the back from scraping on the floor.

CUTTING EDGE

The Predator drone's top speed is 135 miles (217 km) per hour. The X-43A UAV holds the world record drone speed at 7,000 miles (11,265 km) per hour. This drone must be carried up into the air by a large airplane and then released when it is moving fast. It has a scramjet engine that uses fast air moving through it to take the X-43A to its top speeds.

U.S. AIR FORCE

When the Global Hawk drone is cruising along at the same altitude and moving ahead in a straight line, both the ailerons on its wings are closed.

CHAPTER 3

KEEPING WATCH

The ability to keep watch from above is an essential part of modern security work. That is why drones are important pieces of equipment used by the military, police, and other security forces around the world.

SPY DRONES

Security drones are usually small multicopters about the size of a suitcase or smaller. This makes them portable, which means that the military can carry them near to where they will be deployed. Sometimes drones pack away in pieces that need to be assembled before use. Such drones have small motors that make little noise as they spin the rotors. Operators fly the drone over the area that needs to be watched and view live images on a computer screen. The operator can make the drone hover in one position or even land on a rooftop or other vantage point to keep watch over long periods.

CUTTING EDGE

Images and footage from today's high-resolution drone cameras can be analyzed by powerful computers to recognize known criminals or specific people. This facial recognition software can recognize subjects based on anything from nose shape and freckles to facial expressions. The expressions might show that the people being watched are anxious or full of rage. Individuals can also be recognized based on how they walk or their hairstyles!

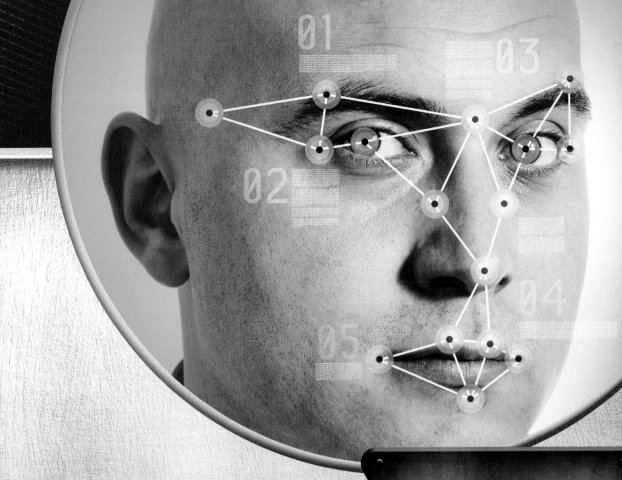

PAYLOADS

To keep watch you need more than just a high-resolution camera. To find people hiding inside darkened buildings or attempting to illegally cross borders at night, a thermal imaging camera is essential. These cameras can detect the infrared radiation, or heat rays, given off by living things. Once drones spot criminals in particular locations, ground forces can move in to make their arrests.

Security forces may use facial recognition software to analyze the film from drones. This measures distances and angles between facial parts to spot particular people's faces.

Surveillance means to carefully watch a suspected criminal or a place where criminal activity might occur. This is an important part of law enforcement because police officers can stop criminals in the act and collect evidence that can lead to arrests. Surveillance is becoming a job for drones.

ON DUTY

Drones are smaller and harder to spot than police officers or helicopters. They can operate for hours at a time, as long as their batteries are recharged, without the need for rest, food, or the restroom! Drones can take direct routes when they are, for example, following a stolen vehicle. They do not need to follow highways and obey traffic lights. They can use thermal imaging cameras that detect heat so that operators can fly at night and "see" where they are going.

DRONE DANGER

In January 2015, a quadcopter illegally landed on the White House lawn and in April of the same year, a drone with traces of radiation landed on the roof of the Japanese prime minister's residence. Neither incident was a real danger, but they do highlight how drones carrying payloads can threaten national security. A new system being developed by police forces in the United States will use a powerful **electromagnetic** beam to take over radio control of a drone and allow security forces to land it in a safe place.

Drones are becoming part of the crime-busting equipment used by police forces.

RESCUE

POLICE DRONES

Drones are operational in police and security forces around the globe, from India and the United Kingdom to North America. In North Dakota, the Grand Forks police department uses drones to fly above crime or road traffic accident scenes to take photographs that might be useful as evidence and to search for people. In one mission, thermal imaging cameras on drones were successfully used to find criminals hiding among tall corn plants in a field. Only around 12 U.S. police departments are equipped and trained to use drones. In many other states, drones are not licensed because people think they might be used by the government to illegally spy on them.

Drones are part of the day-to-day portable kit of modern military forces. Military **reconnaissance** drones are sometimes small multicopters. Some, such as the Black Hornet, are small enough to fit in the palm of an adult hand. Others are bigger, sturdier airplane-shaped drones with greater flying ranges for longer reconnaissance missions. These planes need powerful thrust to make them airborne but usually have only small, light motors. Some are fired into the air on launchers, but many are thrown into the air like a paper dart. Some airplane drones have motors that start when soldiers shake them in their hand before launching! Once in the air, the drones need little power to keep gliding.

RAVEN

The most widespread small military airplane drone in use today is called the Raven. It is carried in pieces in tough cases in troops' backpacks, and can be snapped together in minutes. The Raven has a wingspan of 4.5 feet (1.5 m) and its batteries can power its motor for up to 6.5 miles (10 km) of flight. It has regular and thermal imaging cameras mounted on a device that keeps it from shaking so that it can transmit clear images back to the operators, day or night. The Raven can be flown remotely or can automatically follow routes that are programmed into its flight controller, including returning to base if it is in danger of being shot down. This drone lands by swooping down close to the ground and **stalling** so it stops in midair. Then it drops safely to the ground for reuse.

The autonomous and huge Fire Scout drone has a rotor that is 35 feet (10.7 m) across.

CUTTING EDGE

One of the biggest military surveillance drones is a full-size helicopter named the Fire Scout. Its windows are covered, as it has no pilot! It can take off and land autonomously, usually on naval ships or specially prepared sites on land. It can fly for 12 hours at up to 16,000 feet (4,880 m) above the ground and its future payloads will include equipment for locating enemy craft and hidden mines, or bombs beneath the ground.

CHAPTER 4

IN BATTLES

Military drone airplanes make up a robot air force of awesome power and capabilities. These drones can do anything from tracking the enemy in preparation for combat, to actually attacking ground forces, either using the weapons they carry or by acting as weapons themselves!

The biggest drone in military use is the Global Hawk developed for the U.S. Air Force. It is 44 feet (13 m) long and 15 feet (4.5 m) tall with a wingspan of 116 feet (35 m).

A Global Hawk is maneuvered on the runway by a truck. The curved head of the Hawk contains its navigation equipment and payload.

CUTTING EDGE

In the natural world, bees can swarm and attack enemies that might destroy their hives. The U.S. Navy has already tested Locust drones that swarm in a similar way. Once in flight, the Locusts communicate with one another autonomously and then fly in formation to attack targets using their onboard weapons!

The Global Hawk is built for endurance flights of 32 hours or more at heights up to 50,000 feet (15.2 km) and is controlled by a computer mouse on the ground. Global Hawk's payload includes **radar** and both regular and infrared cameras mounted inside its nose. It flies high gathering intelligence that may be useful for attacks. In the conflict in Syria, in 2015, U.S. Air Force Global Hawks provided information that helped battle planners identify friendly and enemy forces and track the movement of enemy equipment.

DRONE MISSILE

The Switchblade drone is 2 feet (60 cm) long and weighs just over 5 pounds (2 kg). It is fired from a mortar, a type of gun, at concealed enemies. Unlike a regular mortar shell, the shell of the drone has wings that flip out from its sides once in the air. Color and infrared cameras at the front are used to guide the Switchblade while searching for the enemy. It can fly around until it is ready to strike and explode, or even return safely to base if the mission is canceled.

The Predator is by far the most widely used strike drone in the world today. It is part of a tried-and-tested unmanned aircraft system. This includes not only the drones themselves, but also control stations and satellite uplink vehicles.

COMMUNICATION

Operators launch Predators from the ground using joysticks in a ground control station. This can be a mobile station near the battlefield or at an airbase thousands of miles away. The drone is controlled by radio signals from the station until it is out of sight. When the drone is farther away, the control signals are bounced between satellite uplink vehicles and communications satellites in space until they reach the drone.

WEAPONS AND TARGETS

The regular weapons payload of the Predator is Hellfire missiles, which are mounted under each wing. These rockets can travel at 995 miles (1,591 km) per hour carrying about 20 pounds (9 kg) of explosives to their targets. Beneath the Predator's nose is a ball that fires pulses of **laser** and infrared beams at a target identified by GPS. The locations that the pulses hit are detected by laser sensors in the missiles. A computer on the Predator uses the beam to calculate the distance and path the missiles must fly to hit the target.

POWER

The Predator's thrust comes from a Rotax 914F engine that turns a single rotor at the back of the drone. The engine is fuelled by 600 pounds (272 kg) of aircraft fuel stored in fuel bladders balanced on either side of the wings. Batteries provide backup power for the engine if the drone runs out of fuel.

A Predator drone is built to search and destroy military targets from the air.

PREDATOR BODY

To keep the Predator lightweight, it is made from a mixture of light-but-strong materials including foam and Kevlar, a material usually used for bulletproof vests. The wings have tough titanium edges dotted with tiny holes that leak antifreeze to keep ice from building up on the wings and adding weight.

FIGHTER DRONE

One of the most sophisticated drone fighter airplanes in the world is the U.S. Navy's X-47B. It was built to demonstrate the ability of an unmanned aircraft to land on and be launched from moving aircraft carriers, ships from which airplanes can take off and land.

STEALTHY DRONE

The X-47B is a small drone airplane shaped a little like a jagged boomerang. It can fly fast and change direction rapidly. It is ideal for dodging enemy missiles and airplanes, and can carry 4,500 pounds (2,040 kg) of missiles. The drone is not easily spotted by radar as it has stealth features. These features include flat surfaces and sharp edges, which reflect radar much less than rounded, conventional airplanes. It is coated with materials that absorb radar rather than bounce it back. In addition, the engine outlet is small and on top of the plane so that heat sensors on the ground cannot easily detect the heat it produces.

OCEAN OPERATION

Operating from an aircraft carrier is difficult even for a piloted airplane. At sea there are strong winds, waves that move the carrier up and down, and spray or waves hitting the decks. Pilots usually rely on air-traffic controllers who give descriptions of weather and deck conditions and landing signal officers who guide them in using light and hand signals. The X-47B operates autonomously because this information is sent to it in computer code as radio signals. The drone downloads the carrier's position, speed, and pitch from sensors on the ship 100 times every second and adjusts its path to match. It takes off using a catapult launcher from the deck.

The crew on deck watch as the X-47B fighter drone demonstrates taking off from a U.S. aircraft carrier in the Atlantic Ocean.

CUTTING EDGE

In 2015, the X-47B became the first UAV to autonomously refuel itself in midair! It flew just behind a Boeing 707 fuel airplane trailing a long pipe. The X-47B maneuvered until the pipe fit into a fuel socket. Then it transmitted a signal to the fuel plane to allow 4,000 pounds (1,815 kg) of fuel to flow into the drone.

CHAPTER 5

HELP FROM DRONES

Drones can provide useful assistance and information for a wide variety of purposes, helping people in often surprising ways. Drones are used to provide accurate data, quickly and cost-effectively, to help environmentalists, to respond to emergencies, and even to help farmers and miners!

INFORMATION SYSTEMS

Drones are becoming increasingly important for geographic information systems (GIS). A GIS is a computer system that collects, stores, and displays

From the air, drones can survey, study, and map anything from natural features and wildlife to the remains of civilizations.

ROCK SECRETS

Archeologists also use satellite imagery, but because drones fly nearer to the ground, they are better at photographing small features, such as details on rock carvings. Rock carvings can unlock secrets to life thousands of years ago. The use of satellite imagery is also affected by cloud cover, which is not the case when using a drone.

information about the locations of streets, buildings, rivers, and other features on Earth's surface. The great thing about GIS is that people can select the types of data to be shown on a map. One GIS map could show places that produce pollution, such as factories, and sites that can be damaged by pollution, such as streams, to see which streams might be at risk. GIS drones take accurate images of different sites on the ground and convert them into maps and 3-D models.

DRONES FOR ARCHEOLOGY

Drones can even help archeologists unlock the secrets of ancient cultures. Many new archeological discoveries are made in wild, remote places that have not yet been dug up or built on, such as deserts. These regions would take years for a team of archeologists to study. Now, drones can fly close to the ground, record features, and take images that can form detailed, 3-D maps of a landscape in which people lived thousands of years ago. Suddenly what looked like blocks of natural stone are revealed by drone images to be the remains of collapsed temples or burial grounds.

After a disaster, such as a hurricane or earthquake, drones can fly over the affected area and supply an almost instant overview of the damage caused. This gives aid workers an idea of what help is needed.

SAVING LIVES

In November 2013, Typhoon Haiyan devastated an area of the Philippines almost 100 miles (160 km) wide. Entire towns were destroyed and more than 1 million people lost their homes. Aid, such as food and medical supplies, started coming in immediately, but it was difficult to get help to where it was needed because roads and communication systems had been destroyed by the typhoon. Using detailed images sent back by a Global Hawk drone, aid workers found an undamaged airport that could be used as an operations base. The drone helped rescuers find survivors by sending back images of HELP signs and by assessing which roads and routes rescuers could take to get to them.

MONITORING

Making sure enough aid gets to the right places is vitally important. Drones can supply the accurate geographic information needed to make this happen. The numbers of people in refugee camps can change rapidly. Drones can map refugee camps weekly to show how they are growing or shrinking, so that deliveries of aid can be adjusted accordingly. Drones can also produce three-dimensional (3-D) maps that show how an area might be vulnerable to disasters such as floods. This allows aid workers to plan ways to prevent disaster, such as building flood walls or improving sewage systems to ensure excess water drains away before causing a flood.

CUTTING EDGE

Beach lifeguards could soon be using drones for ocean rescues. Ryptide lifeguard drones are designed for rescuing swimmers in distress. These drones will carry and drop four inflatable rings near a swimmer in trouble in fewer than 30 seconds after locating them. The rings inflate automatically as soon as they hit the water. Swimmers can then stay afloat until rescuers arrive.

Drones help emergency and aid workers respond quickly to disasters and help them plan relief efforts.

In order to figure out which animals are in trouble or how best to help an endangered species, scientists must collect large amounts of data. Drones are ideal for this work. Unlike people, drones do not scare animals because they fly almost silently above them. Drones can be used at any time and in any location, and they can produce information about a wide variety of targets.

DRONE TRACKERS

Sometimes biologists track animals to understand how they live and the size of the territory they need to survive. This can be difficult when animals live in dense jungles or remote regions. There is also a risk that if the animals see people or their equipment they may not behave normally, and this would affect any findings. Using drones, biologists can study animals and their habitat easily and safely, without disturbing the wildlife. Drones can carry different cameras depending on the work they need to do. Thermal imaging drones have already been used to count orangutan nests in treetops that otherwise would be obscured from view by leaves.

SAVING WILDLIFE

Drones are being used in the war against hunters and poachers who kill endangered species for sport or to sell. Some conservation societies use drones with cameras above areas where illegal hunting takes place. This allows wardens to check on animals over larger areas than they could check on foot. Because the drones are small and very quiet, poachers do not notice them. By recording their activity on camera, law enforcement officers gain evidence of illegal activities by particular poachers.

Scientists in Canada used a drone's data with a GIS system to make accurate maps of the seals' locations.

COUNTING SEALS

In 2015, scientists studying gray seal colonies in eastern Canada used a drone carrying a thermal imaging camera to survey population numbers and their locations. Even though it was freezing cold and very windy, the team completed the work in just two days. The seals' warm bodies showed up easily against the cold landscape.

NATURAL RESOURCES

We rely on natural resources for many of the things we use every day. Some, such as coal, are used almost unprocessed. Others are processed in some way to be made useful. Around the world, drones are increasingly being used to improve the amount of resources produced or found.

MINING MATTERS

Mining operations can cover hundreds of miles, which means that it takes a long time to assess remaining resource amounts. Putting people into a pit to check resources is also dangerous. Flying drones over and into open pits to measure the amount of rock extracted from an area, and check its condition, is both safer and quicker. Drones can also be used to fly close to cliffs that have been blasted with explosives to create mining pits to find out if any have not exploded. Drones are being used in the oil and gas industry, too, to inspect rigs. In the past, to inspect high towers people had to climb them. Now, drones can go up, take a look, and then come down in a process that is safe, quick, and cheap.

FARM DRONES

Many farms cover huge areas of land, meaning that farmers waste a lot of time traveling to check on their crops and animals. Drones can fly over fields and detect signs of crop disease, insect pests, or sick animals much more quickly than human observers. The drones carry different sensors depending on the type of survey they are carrying out. Some sensors measure areas with a green color to assess the maturity of crop plants. Other sensors measure moisture levels to tell a farmer which fields need watering.

CUTTING EDGE

In the future, more and more farmers will use drones to spray land with chemicals such as fertilizer and herbicide. The drones carry a tank that contains liquid spray. They are more fuel-efficient and accurate in distributing the chemicals than a regular crop-spraying plane. The drones use radar to scan the ground and ensure they stay the optimum distance from crops and spray the correct amount of liquid.

Low-flying drones can check the health of crops in large fields and the data they collect can help farmers make decisions about spraying their plants.

CHAPTER 6

DRONES EVERYWHERE

Experts predict that the market for nonmilitary drones will increase by nearly 20 percent between 2015 and 2020, four times faster than the military market.

TAKING FLIGHT

The major industries to use drones will be agriculture, energy, mining, construction, real estate, news media, and movie production. There will be changes to the laws soon to make drone use legal. By 2017, regulations should allow commercial drone flights in the United States without a license, at low altitude, and within view of the operators.

Drones are probably for sale in a mall toy or gadget store near you. Each year they are becoming less and less expensive to buy.

CUTTING EDGE

Soon, the cartoon characters that you might see at a theme park may take to the air to make their parades and displays more spectacular. Disney plans to use drones to make floating models for use in parades. Tiny drones may move the long limbs of large characters such as Jack Skellington from *The Nightmare Before Christmas* or make parts of a building explode through the air in slow motion.

LEISURE DRONES

Global estimates are that 1 million drones were given as gifts in 2015. Look online and you will see how easy it is to buy a drone for leisure purposes today. One of the current top leisure drones is the Parrot BeBop. Costing around $500, this drone has a high-resolution fisheye camera, whose images are easily sent to a tablet or smartphone, or even to virtual reality goggles so you feel like you are flying! The drone can fly for 22 minutes at up to 984 feet (300 m) from the controller. It has soft plastic rotors that stop rotating if they hit anything, to prevent injury or damage. In 2016, a new automatic drone called Lily Camera hit the market. To operate the drone, it must be thrown into the air where it automatically flies behind and films the user. It does this by tracking a GPS bracelet that the user wears.

What do *Captain America*, *Skyfall*, and the Harry Potter movies have in common? They were all partly filmed with drones.

AERIAL FOOTAGE

Drones are currently big news in moviemaking right now for several reasons. They give moviemakers an aerial point of view. They can look down on the action, spin around a subject, and move through small spaces. These shots can be achieved in real spaces without the need to make elaborate and expensive artificial sets though which cameras on trolleys can move. Using drones is less expensive than using helicopters for all aerial work. It is estimated that the day rate for a helicopter plus movie crew is up to $40,000 but costs just $15,000 for the equivalent drone service. Until 2014, moviemakers were not licensed to shoot with drones in the United States and United Kingdom, so drone footage was shot in other countries where it was legal. A rooftop motorbike chase sequence in *Skyfall* was filmed in Istanbul, Turkey. As laws change, there will be more and more drone sequences in movies.

RANGE OF MOVIES

Drones are increasingly being used to shoot many different types of shorter sequences, including commercials and movies promoting events and products. Broadcasts of sporting events, such as snowboarding and skiing events at the 2015 Winter Olympics, were enhanced by drones filming close to the performers. Some wedding venues now license drone filming of their clients' weddings, but do not recommend use during the quiet ceremony itself owing to the whirring noise of the rotors!

CUTTING EDGE

In 2016, the first feature-length movie to be filmed entirely using cameras on drones will begin shooting. *Final Minute* is a crime thriller set in Ecuador. The movie will be shot using DJI Inspire drones. These are amongst the smallest, easiest to use professional aerial moviemaking drones available. They have very high-quality digital cameras with which to capture the shots.

"Dronies," or photos and movies you take of yourself using a drone, are the new "selfies"!

The remarkable drones that are flying in the skies today have only been made possible by the work of inventors. They have researched and developed new systems to control and improve drone flight, carry different payloads, and make drone operation easier. Inventors look for inspiration to meet the challenges of future drone design, and one of these is the natural world. When designers copy natural solutions to mechanical problems, it is called biomimicry.

BEE EYES

The SenseFly drone, developed at Lausanne Institute of Technology in Switzerland, uses a video system inspired by bumblebees. As a bee flies closer to an object, the images it sees reload more quickly in order to bring them into focus. The bee calculates when to avoid the approaching object based on the speed of the image reloading. The SenseFly's processor works in the same way to automatically avoid objects and avoid collisions.

SWAN NECKS

When swans fly, their bodies shift up and down as they beat their large wings. Yet their heads remain stable in a fixed position. Researchers at Stanford University analyzed how swans do this by stiffening and flexing bones and muscles in their necks to cancel out the movements. It is a natural image stabilizer. The researchers then designed a suspension system using springs that could allow drones to record steadier video during flight.

BAT WINGS

Bats are sophisticated fliers. They can avoid obstacles when flying in tight spaces and recover rather than crash if they do touch something. Drone researchers at the U.S. Navy observed bats in slow-motion movies and discovered that they can fold up their wings to avoid objects and then lock again to flap and glide. The researchers developed a drone with folding wings that flies like a bat. It does not even crash if hit with a metal rod!

The developers of Sensefly drones observed how flying insects see the world around them to help them make systems allowing their robots to fly near the ground and avoid objects.

FUTURE DRONES

At a trade fair in Las Vegas in early 2016, a Chinese company unveiled a drone that can carry a human passenger. Ehang Inc. claim that this invention is a world first. Their electric quadcopter has room for one person and a backpack and was designed to fly for 23 minutes at heights of around 1,000 feet (300 m).

GETTING CONNECTED

In some parts of the world, people cannot get Internet access because there is a lack of telephone wires and cell phone towers. Titan Aerospace is developing drones the size of passenger airplanes that have **solar panels** on top of their wings. The panels power nonstop flight at high altitude around the globe. The drones would be used to bounce wireless Internet data from transmitters in one part of Earth to areas that need it.

RESCUE

The GimBall drone made by Flyability is designed to work in disaster areas to search for human survivors. It is the world's first drone that is tolerant of collisions and uses them to find its way, a little like how insects

CUTTING EDGE

In Singapore, Malaysia, owners of a large restaurant are using a fleet of drone waiters to deliver food! The quadcopters navigate using infrared sensors and can carry up to 4.4 pounds (2 kg) each. The reason they need drones is that there are fewer people who want to be waiters in restaurants in Malaysia.

change course if they fly into a window. This drone has a rotating frame with the rotor and camera mounted inside out of harm's way.

DELIVERIES

Amazon and Google see a future in which people order goods on the Internet and expect them to be delivered within hours by drone. Google has tested prototype drones in Australia, delivering cattle medicine and chocolate by hovering over the destination and lowering the cargo by cable to avoid needing to land.

How soon will it be before drones like this will be able to deliver express parcels?

Drones are part of the robotics revolution that is transforming daily lives around our planet and beyond. Robots are helping us explore oceans and space, carry out highly accurate surgeries, and build cars and other objects faster and with less danger to humans.

RISING ROBOTS

Drones are helping us get better views from above for any kind of filming. Their use has transformed aerial warfare and their adaptability is helping different activities, from disaster relief and conservation to moviemaking. Using drones can make many tasks safer because the operators remain safely on the ground, or the drones fly autonomously.

The use of drones has taken off and is gradually transforming industries and lives worldwide.

CUTTING EDGE

When a rogue drone is on the loose causing danger, it is time to call in a drone catcher! A research team at the Michigan Technological University has developed a drone that can shoot a large net at a rogue drone up to 40 feet (12 m) away, wrap it up, and lift it up and away to a safe place.

SOLVING PROBLEMS

Marcel Hirscher had a very lucky escape when he took part in an Alpine slalom ski event at a World Cup race in late 2015. A drone being used to film his run crashed inches behind him. One of the biggest problems in using drones is that they can cause serious damage when they stop working properly, lose control, or run out of power. Designers are already making drones with rotors that cause less damage by being made of softer materials or protected by cages, or that carry on flying even if they hit something. In addition, newer generations of batteries are being developed that can store more power for longer operation, not only of drones, but also other autonomous robots. Drone use is controversial in some places, but with careful regulation, their use can spread for the benefit of a wide range of industries worldwide.

GLOSSARY

accelerometers devices for measuring the rate of speed change in moving objects

altimeter a device for measuring height above the ground

autonomous working independently

data information

drag the force of air that pushes against moving objects

electromagnetic a force using the magnetic pushes and pulls caused by electric currents

forces pushes or pulls

global positioning system (GPS) a system used to figure out the position on Earth based on distances from satellites in space

gravity the force that makes things fall toward Earth

gyroscopes devices that measure change of direction and position using gravity

laser a device producing a narrow beam of intense light

payload useful equipment that an aircraft carries

programming giving a machine coded instructions to automatically do a job

radar a system for detecting the presence and location of moving vehicles by detecting the reflections of radio waves

reconnaissance the military observation of enemy forces and defenses

rotors sets of propellers that rotate together

rudder a device that makes a moving object change course

sensors devices that sense things such as heat, distance, speed, or movement

solar panels devices that can convert sunlight into electricity

stalling slowing or stopping

FOR MORE INFORMATION

BOOKS

Ceceri, Kathy. *Robotics: Discover the Science and Technology of the Future with 20 Projects* (Build It Yourself). White River Junction, VT: Nomad Press, 2012.

Drones: From Insect Spy Drones to Bomber Drones. New York, NY: Scholastic, 2014.

Kirby, Terry and Belinda. *Getting Started with Drones: Build and Customize Your Own Quadcopter.* San Francisco, CA: Maker Media, 2015.

Ripley, Tim. *Drone Operators: What It Takes to Join the Elite* (Military Jobs). New York, NY: Cavendish Square Publishing, 2015.

WEBSITES

Learn about some of the ways that drones are being used in conservation at:
blog.arkive.org/2015/07/how-are-drones-being-used-for-conservation

Check out the introduction movie at this link and some of the short movies made using drones at:
www.nycdronefilmfestival.com

Meet some robotic scientists and find out how they landed a career in this industry at:
robotics.nasa.gov/students/robotics.php

INDEX